Wash Your Bowl

Mandy —
Thanks!
I hope you like the poems.
Viva ALC!

2014

Wash Your Bowl

poems

Matthew Falk

© 2014 by Matthew Falk. All rights reserved. Any unauthorized reproduction of this work, in whole or in part, may result in irremediable karmic imbalance.

Designed and typeset by the author in Adobe Garamond Pro and Bell Gothic.

Manufactured by Spencer Printing and Graphics, Honesdale, PA, in a limited edition of 200 copies, of which this is #__8__.

ISBN 978-0-9892390-1-1

Published and distributed by
Satori Resartus Enterprises
Baltimore, USA 21218

*This book is for Shari,
although I hope that You,
whoever you are,
will also enjoy it.*

Tabled Discontent

Aubade	11
Corner of Guilford and 29th St.	12
Imago	13
Unmapped	14
Opus Posthumous	15
I Got This	16
Refuge	18
Charm City Circulator	19
#want	20
Anomiad	21
Noblesse Oblige	22
Super Rural Ambulance, Amended	23
Loop Electrosurgical Excision Procedure	25
How to Recognize Trees in Winter	26
Southern Central Rain	27
Scientists Identify Ten Basic Odors	28

The Singing Lesson	30
New Adventures of Supermoon	31
Easter 2016	33
Threnody	34
The Confession of St. Schwitters	35
Metanymity	37
Autoreply	38
Sit Down and Shut Up	39
This Way to the Egress	40
Ashtray Mouth	41
Marooned	42

The poem must resist the intelligence
　　　Almost successfully.

　　　　　　Wallace Stevens

　　　Here comes two of you.
　　Which one will you choose?

　　　　　　Lou Reed

Aubade

every sunrise is
a warning
i refuse
to heed.
today
will be
briefer than
yesterday.

lately
i'm learning
to begin
at the end,
to work
backwards.
i'm learning
to walk
again.

i talk
to trees.
they listen,
they know
what it's like
to drop
everything,
to stand
naked
as winter
closes in.

Corner of Guilford and 29th St., Tuesday, August 6th, 10 am

On such a day as this one everything
is just as it is. Good morning, you,
drinking Natty Boh on your stoop;
and you, blasting songs of teenage lust
from your double-parked Buick; you, walking
three dogs; you, dogs; you, dead
dragonfly belly-up on the sidewalk;
you, sun that bakes the dragonfly
and turns my face the color of
the fish-killing algae in the harbor;
you, hot wind full of the smell of dead fish;
and you—yes, you!—listen to me:
I know you; I am you. Help me
summon the ghost of Walt Whitman!
Let us raise Walt's effigy
above the Washington Monument,
let us rest together in the shade of his hat!
Let his mighty beard be
Baltimore, and each of us as
unique and interchangeable
as hairs in that beard.

Imago

She named him Frederick
when we found him clinging
to the window screen.
He was dead, almost
as large as my thumb.
I don't know how to know
if he was really a he,
but the act of naming
made it so. He was,
and is, iridescent.
We realized he was dead
only after she observed
he never moved.
He kept holding on,
an affront to the doctrine
of non-attachment.

The Japanese say cicadas
are emblems of reincarnation.
The Chinese eat them.
Americans like us
pluck them from screens
to adorn our hats.
I admired Frederick
for his failure
to decay, his resistance
to rain and sun,
his blank compound eyes,
his prodigious grasping
of whatever surface
presented itself.

Unmapped

Sometimes I fall
through myself
like rooms
in a burning house.

No one speaks
my language.
My words turn
into fingers, my fingers
into flowers.

There is so much work to do:
Wash your bowl,
boil the milk,
unfurl the blank banners,
empty your pockets,
touch no one.

When will I learn
how to fold myself
into a crane
and let the wind
carry me away?

Opus Posthumous

My father's face was nothing
like mine, except for his bad skin
and bad eyes. I will soon be older
than he ever was.
Here is a photo,
dated December 1969:
He is covered in cats.
I can remember the smell
of his pipe tobacco.
I remember he used to read
Omni, the journal of pseudoscience.
I remember seeing his face, preserved
by the embalmer's art, and thinking,
This is not my father,
this is some kind of trick.
I don't remember feeling
sad after the funeral.
And when people would ask me,
What does your dad do?
I would say: Decomposes.
And I never knew why
that wasn't funny.

I Got This

my brain's a screen
door swinging
in the rain
& with all
these bugs
coming in i can't
concentrate on nothing
but this goddamn

buzzing
when i lie
down to sleep
or wake up & walk
there's no
silence

anywhere ever
& in the streets
citizens are sick
with singing
their own
names off
key & i

got this lexical
ague & this
lichen-like
agility i'll give
you if you
help me forget
myself the same way

i forgot how
your fingers used to
make the sign
of the southern
cross under the northern
lights before

your gift
for the givenness
of things dissolved
like halos
into halogen
plumes & how
we once
plumbed sodium

chloride while a
chorus somewhere
mumbled
te deum
laudanum

Refuge

In your letter you say
you killed a couple
of baby mice
with your shovel
while planting trees
at your Buddhist hermitage.

And you say
you're sorry.
But I say
you shouldn't be.

This is simply
how things are.

Before you
could build
the new temple
you had to tear down
the barn
where generations
of spiders
had lived and devoured
generations of flies.

Charm City Circulator

On the bus
or stuck in traffic
we need the electric
ticker tape to feed us
headlines from the *Sun*
because we can't stand
to be alone.
"Truck catches fire on I-95,
driver killed: VIDEO."
Man seated next to me
pulls out his iPhone, and I imagine
he wants to watch that video.
What kind of person
wants to see another person
burning to death?
But as I judge him I'm overcome
by vertigo, and I realize
I want to watch it, too,
but I expect to see my own
face in the flames.
Will it be like
the scene in *Indiana Jones*
when the Nazis open the ark?
Later, when I get home,
I'll call a friend and say
something mean
and not what I mean
because I'm unable to tell her
I saw both of us
and everyone we know
on fire, it's all over the news.

#want

He wants a gun.
She wants to buy
Xanax online.
He wants to draw
a cat for her.

She wants egg in her beer.
He wants visibility.
She wants to name her son Lucifer.
He wants to find out
the history of her house.

She wants to keep an open
bug bite moist.
He wants to see
how animals eat.
She wants a physicist
to speak at his funeral.

Anomiad

desire put her finger
down her throat
and up came the world

but the world turned
out to be boring

so she went
to the movies
with death
and they snuck in

a fifth of raspberry vodka
then had sloppy sex
in death's car

and desire conceived
me: not yet born,
i'm already bored

Noblesse Oblige

So this gang
of blue-hairs
all dressed up
like Madonna rolls
into Mondawmin Mall
on tall white unicycles
with tarot cards
between the spokes.
Keening "O Mio
Babbino Caro,"
they joust with their
jewel-encrusted
wrought-iron canes.
All the shoppers
put down their bags
to wager on the tournament,
but no one can
figure out the rules
so no one knows who wins.
Afterwards, the women,
on their way out,
pocket the pennies
from the water feature,
throw rhubarb tarts
at the security cameras,
and overturn every
SUV in the parking lot.

APPEARANCE:

Individuals described in this section are individuals. The uniform does not promulgate regulations or provide criteria for determining whether a structure is described, nor does it account for an inability to perform two or more activities of daily living.

LANGUAGE:

Here there are authorized to be carried out evidence-based, demographically appropriate messages, presented in a linguistically sensitive manner. Ongoing face-to-face, telephonic or web-based intervention shall establish the most current minimum intervals other than those efforts which adversely impact the safe use of the drug.

POTENTIALLY MISVALUED WORK CODES:

The relative validation of work units shall include a sampling of codes:

Codes (and families of codes as appropriate) for which there has been the fastest growth; codes (and families of codes as appropriate) that have experienced substantial changes in practice; codes for new technologies or services within an appropriate period after the relative values are initially established for such codes; codes with low relative values; codes which have not been subject to review since implementation (the so-called "Harvard-valued codes").

Rules of Construction:

Nothing in this section shall be construed. Nothing in this section shall be described in the preceding sections.

Termination of Authority:

Strike "at the option of the State, provide" and insert "provide, at the option of the State." Strike "Option for Children." Strike $100,000,000 and insert $0. Strike $22,290,000,000 and insert $0. Strike $10,000 and insert $13,170.

Anti-Avoidance Guidance:

Absence of caregivers. Language barriers. Atypical transportation costs.

Exclusion of Phototherapy:

Strike and insert the following flush sentence:

Loop Electrosurgical Excision Procedure

we sewed you up
like a purse
said the nurse
clasping an invisible
handbag

her smile
was fixed
her simile
reminded you
you were broke
and losing
a day's pay

after the smoke
and the smell of you
burning cleared
they showed you
the piece of flesh
they'd taken

when you told me
it was as big
as my finger
did you mean
to point
out the blood
on my hands

How to Recognize Trees in Winter

I have reached
that moonless age when
everything haunts me.

In the shrunken sky,
gray-faced spacemen
with too many teeth
remind me of everyone
I have never been.

In the garden of salt,
all the lights are on.

I spend my days
smashing radios, driving
nails into loaves of bread,
inventing names for new
colors. Home is just
where we left it.

Southern Central Rain

1.

I'm sorry I lied, I pretended
to admire your poetry.
I'm sorry I reminded you
when I met you at Penn Station
in my favorite hat
of your father, whom you hate.
I'm sorry for laughing
at everything, for my lack
of gravitas. I'm sorry I don't like
arguing, never have
any money, can't understand
French, and don't believe
in anything. I'm sorry for writing
so many poems about you
I never let you read.

2.

I forgive you for taking
everything seriously.
I forgive you for your family
and your narcissism.
I forgive you for hating
Baltimore, having bad taste in music,
and watching television all day.
I forgive your poetry.
I forgive you for seeing through me
and never trying
to tell me
a single white lie.

Scientists Identify Ten Basic Odors

1: Sleep

Sleep smells like an abandoned hardware store. Like fennel. Like static electricity. And it's full of reasons. Colorless green ideas sleep furiously.

2: Cities

Eastern cities smell deep indigo. As you move west the smell becomes more like math. Cities rarely smell like their names. The smell of a city includes crows, both feral and domestic; chrome and glass; empty rooms; lost lovers.

3: Teeth

Guitars, eyelashes, and shekels. Joshu's oak in the garden.

4: Water

We may be in over our heads here.

5: Trees

The odor of trees is completely different from sweaters, boots, sages, mushrooms, or Scandinavia. Think of a rhombus with fewer or more than four sides. That is not a tree. The plural of rhombus is rhombi. O come, o come, Emmanuel.

6: Music

[*this space intentionally left blank*]

7: Films

Overheard:

As soon as we started
Shooting the neighbor
Decided to get in on it.

8: Skin

You might think skin would smell like water, or trees. You would be half right.

9: Semioticians

You're on a train stalled somewhere in West Virginia during a thunderstorm. It is either very late at night or very early in the morning. The power has gone out. The doors won't open. Everyone is drunk and the washroom is always occupied because there's nowhere else to smoke.

10: Walkie-Talkies

They smell like spiders. No one knows why. The dream of a universal language.

The Singing Lesson

Your voice is fine,
she says,
when it's soft.

But you're using
the wrong vowels,
and they make your face
look like this:

No, look.
Like this:

That face is
why you sound
like some weird kind of
wounded animal.

New Adventures of Supermoon

Today I'm remembering
the largest moon of the year.
I'd like to write a poem
about how it followed us
from New York into Ontario
as if it knew we'd never
get another chance
to look at it together,
how it appeared to me
without my glasses
as a great bright blob,
a future-shaped hole
in the empty sky.
But I don't know how
to put the moon in a poem
without saying the same things
everyone has already said.
What if I use a word
such as "perigee"—
will its scientific precision
save the poem
from sentimentality?
Or will science discover
the problem is the poem
doesn't want to be
about the moon?
It wants to be about how it felt
to sleep with her
for the last time,
our bodies at perigee, our blood
made of the same
substance as the salty tides

that rise and fall
like breathing
at the moon's command.
The poem wants
to be about waking up
next to her into
my real life at last,
about the joy and the suffering
of the world.
But there's even less that's new
to say about that
than there is about the moon.

Easter 2016

I met a man who sells
second-hand tourniquets
to Gideons and gutterpunks.
His spirit animal
is the centipede.

Another man sleeps
on a pallet in an empty
warehouse. His radio,
tuned to static, tells him
what God wants.

A woman lurks in bus shelters,
humming and holding out
shoeboxes full of bones.
Once, she says, she dreamed
she had a secret name but can't
remember now what it was.

Threnody

You'd been gone three days
when we found your car
in the forest
a mile from the road.
The keys were in the ignition,
your clothes were on the seat,
and your footprints led us
to the edge of a cliff,
so I said you must have
learned how to fly.

And when we bore your
three hundred pound frame
in another hundred
pounds of pine,
your brother said
it would have been easier
if you had died
of starvation.

And while your widow
flirted with the undertakers
and the rented eulogist
kept calling you
by the wrong name,
we argued
about who would get
your guns and where
to go for a drink.

The Confession of St. Schwitters

From the universality of contradiction, I shall proceed to the particularity of contradiction. In ancient times, at the assembly on Spiritual Mountain, Buddha picked up a flower and showed it to the crowd. Hegel's assertion that art was once the adequate stage of spirit and now no longer is, demonstrates a trust in the real progress of consciousness that has since been bitterly disappointed. Or what way do I have of knowing that if I say I don't know something I don't really in fact know it?

The mind/body problem can be posed sensibly only insofar as we have a definite conception of body. There is an old legend that once it was the women who "owned" the molimo, but the men stole it from them and ever since the women have been forbidden to see it. If such difficulties could come into existence, something must be wrong with our teaching system. In the room the women come and go, talking of Michelangelo.

The man who cries out with pain, or says that he has pain, doesn't choose the mouth which says it. Do you understand that understanding is impossible? In all languages it is the smallest and most innocent-looking words which have given rise to the most trouble. *Cada palabra de la voz del radio es una mentira.*

This is not the place to give even in outline a theory of violence and its role in history. Rapid motion through space elates one; so does notoriety; so does the possession of money. "Shut up, Bobby Lee," The Misfit said. "It's no real pleasure in life." As we have seen, the situation of the world is so complex that one can not fight everywhere at the same time and for everyone.

The sublunary realm, the terrestrial cesspool, is here likened to a cattle-pen. Did he who made the Lamb make thee? Certainly, there is a way to escape the effects of earthly gravitation, by using a powerful rocket that overshoots the critical point of terrestrial attraction, but I cannot see how music's less harmful projectiles could ever reach this point or its imaginary equivalent.

Metanymity

My name is neither
a mansion nor a bomb.
Sometimes it sounds
like snow, sometimes
like locusts.
At night I know
my name dreams of me.
I hope it dies
when I do, leaving
only a quick light
breath, like you take
in the middle of a long
kiss.

Autoreply

She calls me from San Francisco,
her voice full of fog
and the Pacific's vast,
inscrutable self-reliance.
I recall pressing mollusk shells
up to my ear as a boy
and pretending the noise in my head
was an ancient transmission
from Panthalassa,
or at least Lake Superior.
My father once told me
it was the sound of my blood,
but he was wrong.
On the west coast
it's always three hours ago,
the day forever full of promise,
but here it's the end
of another long afternoon
of not knowing
who I am when I'm alone.

Sit Down and Shut Up

The clock in the meditation room
comes and goes.
Of course that's impossible;
only the clock
in the mind can do that.
It's the same
with the bodies
fidgeting around you,
the upstairs conversation
on the maddening edge
of being understood, the Sunday
hum of Midtown traffic:
they come and go,
just like you. Who is it
who notices when you are gone,
and when you return?
Once when a student complained
he could not concentrate
because the local villagers
had kept him awake
with their all-night revelry,
Ajahn Chah rebuked him thus:
"Why do you say the noise
disturbs you? Is it not you
who are disturbing the noise?"

This Way to the Egress

Across the alley the policemen
dance, elegant as gardens,
possible as gray houses.

We are too busy
verbing the children's nouns to care
if journalists clamor for instant
jets or carrion orchestras.

Every bird is not a pigeon.
Not all our words come from
television. Autonomy:
memento mori.

Our hearts are full of the smell
and the color of October. Let's sing
with our mouths full of rain.

Ashtray Mouth

I swear, she makes me want to change my name.
When she puts on that face, I understand
what the world is for. She never makes demands
because she knows there's no such thing as time.
Mornings, over coffee, while I slowly
assemble fragments of my consciousness,
she talks to me about her dreams. I kiss
her with my ashtray mouth, then in my holey
socks and wrinkled shirt I sit and stare
at starlings in the half-dead tree outside;
I watch them gather twigs, try to decide
which twigs are best for nests and whom to share
them with. And when at last I look away,
she's still here, though April's gone and so is May.

Marooned

I fear this door is in fact
a window or a mirror
reflecting itself. Yours
is a face a whore might have
slapped. You've always been
a bad tipper. Those oranges
you zested yesterday
have turned into tiny
moths and swarmed ashore
to be marooned and purpled
in the indelicate heat
of this cancerous tropic.
You'll have to go
crabwise into the mirror
to discover the door
is a trap. Let it draw you
into the toadless garden
we planted and forgot
to water. Waiter,
there's a spy in my suit:
I think he's me.

Disclaimers and Acknowledgments

"#want" is based on results of Google's autofill search function.

"Super Rural Ambulance, Amended" comprises slightly altered excerpts from *H.R. 3590 (111th)*, also known as *The Patient Protection and Affordable Care Act*.

"Scientists Identify Ten Basic Odors" was inspired by a *Baltimore Sun* headline.

"The Confession of St. Schwitters" is a collage of pre-existing texts.

The author is grateful to the editors of the following publications, where versions of some of these poems first appeared (sometimes under different titles):

Artichoke Haircut; The Atticus Review; Barely South Review; The Body Attacks Itself; Cardinal Sins; Everyday Genius; H_NGM_N; Hidden City Quarterly; The Little Patuxent Review; Magic Octopus; Monologging; Plorkology; Smile, Hon, You're in Baltimore!; What Weekly.

Enormous gratitude also goes out to the students, staff, and faculty at the University of Baltimore, without whose support, advice, and encouragement this book would not exist. *Gassho.*

About the Author

Born in Wisconsin in the 1970s, Matthew Falk has lived in Baltimore since 2010. He is a musician, editor, college writing instructor, armchair phenomenologist, and cat person.

*Some words point to things;
others poke you in the eye
and pick your pockets.*

Index

Animals, 12, 15, 18, 20, 30, 33, 36

Birds, 14, 28, 40, 41
Bugs, 12, 13, 16, 18, 20, 29, 33, 37, 42
Buses, 19, 33

Children, 24, 40

Faces, 12, 15, 19, 23, 26, 30, 41, 42
Fingers, 14, 17, 21, 25

Gardens, 26, 40, 42

Hats, 12, 13, 27
Houses, 14, 20, 37, 40

Money, 22, 24, 25, 27, 28, 36

Radios, 26, 33, 35
Rain, 13, 16, 27, 40

Salt, 17, 26, 31
Science, 15, 20, 28, 31
Sleep, 16, 28, 31, 33
Sun, 11, 12, 13, 19

Telephones, 19, 23, 38
Trees, 11, 18, 28, 41

Unicycles, 22

Work, 11, 14, 23